50 Quick Ways to S

By Mike Gershon

Text Copyright © 2017 Mike Gershon

All Rights Reserved

About the Author

Mike Gershon is an expert educationalist who works throughout the UK and abroad helping teachers to develop their practice. His knowledge of teaching and learning is rooted in the practicalities of the classroom and his online teaching tools have been viewed and downloaded more than 3.5 million times, making them some of the most popular of all time.

He is the author of over 80 books and guides covering different areas of teaching and learning. Some of Mike's bestsellers include books on assessment for learning, questioning, differentiation and outstanding teaching, as well as Growth Mindsets. You can train online with Mike, from anywhere in the world, at www.tes.com/institute/cpd-courses-teachers.

You can also find out more at www.mikegershon.com and www.gershongrowthmindsets.com, including about Mike's inspirational in-school training and student workshops.

Training and Consultancy

Mike offers a range of training and consultancy services covering all areas of teaching and learning, raising achievement and classroom practice. He runs inspiring and engaging INSET in primary schools, secondary schools and colleges. Examples of recent training events include:

- Growth Mindsets: Theory and Practice – William Bellamy Primary School, Dagenham
- Creating a Challenge Culture: Stretch and Challenge Reimagined – Manchester College
- Rethinking Differentiation – The British School of Brussels

To find out more, visit www.mikegershon.com or www.gershongrowthmindsets.com or get in touch via mike@mikegershon.com

Other Works from the Same Author

Available to buy now on Amazon:

How to Develop Growth Mindsets in the Classroom: The Complete Guide

How to use Differentiation in the Classroom: The Complete Guide

How to use Assessment for Learning in the Classroom: The Complete Guide

How to use Bloom's Taxonomy in the Classroom: The Complete Guide

How to use Questioning in the Classroom: The Complete Guide

How to use Discussion in the Classroom: The Complete Guide

How to Manage Behaviour in the Classroom: The Complete Guide

How to Teach EAL Students in the Classroom: The Complete Guide

How to be an Outstanding Trainee Teacher: The Complete Guide

More Secondary Starters and Plenaries

Secondary Starters and Plenaries: History

Teach Now! History: Becoming a Great History Teacher

The Growth Mindset Pocketbook (with Professor Barry Hymer)

The Exams, Tests and Revision Pocketbook

Also available to buy now on Amazon, the entire 'Quick 50' Series:

50 Quick Ways to Get Past 'I Don't Know'

50 Quick Ways to Start Your Lessons with a Bang!

50 Quick Ways to Improve Literacy Across the Curriculum

50 Quick Ways to Improve Feedback and Marking

50 Quick Ways to Use Scaffolding and Modelling

50 Quick Ways to Stretch and Challenge More-Able Students

50 Quick Ways to Create Independent Learners

50 Quick Ways to go from Good to Outstanding

50 Quick Ways to Support Less-Able Learners

50 Quick and Brilliant Teaching Ideas

50 Quick and Brilliant Teaching Techniques

50 Quick and Easy Lesson Activities

50 Quick Ways to Help Your Students Secure A and B Grades at GCSE

50 Quick Ways to Help Your Students Think, Learn, and Use Their Brains Brilliantly

50 Quick Ways to Motivate and Engage Your Students

50 Quick Ways to Outstanding Teaching

50 Quick Ways to Perfect Behaviour Management

50 Quick and Brilliant Teaching Games

50 Quick and Easy Ways Leaders Can Prepare for Ofsted

50 Quick and Easy Ways to Outstanding Group Work

50 Quick and Easy Ways to Prepare for Ofsted

About the Series

The 'Quick 50' series was born out of a desire to provide teachers with practical, tried and tested ideas, activities, strategies and techniques which would help them to teach brilliant lessons, raise achievement and engage and inspire their students.

Every title in the series distils great teaching wisdom into fifty bite-sized chunks. These are easy to digest and easy to apply – perfect for the busy teacher who wants to develop their practice and support their students.

Acknowledgements

My thanks to all the staff and students I have worked with past and present, particularly those at Pimlico Academy and King Edward VI School, Bury St Edmunds. Thanks also to the teachers and teaching assistants who have attended my training sessions and who always offer great insights into what works in the classroom. Finally, thanks to Gordon at Kall Kwik for his design work.

Table of Contents

Introduction 13

Arresting Images 15

Counterintuitive Images 16

Images Which Need Unpicking 17

Unusual Sounds 18

Musical Interlude 19

Record Yourself...20

Record Students 21

Record the Head 22

YouTube 23

Videos From Another World 25

Social Media 26

Text/Tweet Me The Answer.......................................27

A Link, Just a Link 28

Google This!!...29

Snapshot 30

Stingray Questions 31

Why X if Y? 32

Counterfactual Questions 34

BuzzFeed Lists 36

Hidden Questions 37

Doorway Challenge	38
Doorway Questions and Answers	40
Doorway Mission	41
Dress Up	42
Hand Out Props	43
Mystery Objects Await	44
Crime Scene	46
Mystery Lesson	48
Secret Missions on Desks	49
Sit on the Floor	50
Remove the Chairs	52
Remove the Tables	53
Three Envelopes on Each Desk	54
Lucky Dip	56
Fortune Cookies	57
Real-World Problems	58
Compelling Stories	59
Last Night's News	60
Read Aloud	61
Podcast	62
Arrange to Receive a Call	63
Arrange to Receive a Visit	64
Time Limit	65

Multiple Time Limits	66
Procedural Challenges	67
Lesson Start Race	68
Human Jigsaw	69
Team Challenge	70
Sound the Alarm	71
Take it Outside	73
A Brief Request	75

Introduction

Welcome to 50 Quick Ways to Start Your Lessons with a Bang! This book is all about different strategies, activities and techniques you can use to make the beginning of your lessons memorable, exciting and engaging. The aim is to get students motivated and focussed on learning from the moment they enter your room. And there is a big emphasis on having fun and enjoying learning as well.

The fifty entries which follow contain a wide range of different ideas. Many look at how introducing something novel, or changing the familiar routine, can be a great way to energise students and play on their natural curiosity. Variety, after all, is the spice of life.

To help illustrate how the ideas work in practice, I've provided two examples for each one. This means that every entry has a brief introduction outlining the idea, followed by two demonstrations of how it works.

I've used examples from different subjects and age groups to show how the ideas can be applied in all sorts of different settings. You can use the majority of them in the majority of subjects and with a wide range of different age groups. As ever, nothing is set in stone. You can take the ideas, adapt them, modify them and make them your own. I'm sure as you read through you'll also think of your own ideas – sparked off by some of the things you come across.

All in all then, this book is intended as a highly practical pocketbook you can turn to whenever you want to try something different at the start of your lessons. I'm sure you and your students will have fun trying out some of the ideas.

Arresting Images

01 Images can fire the imagination by showing the world in a different light. Arresting images make students think again. They take hold of the start of your lesson and say: 'What about this? How can we make sense of it?'

Example 1: In a maths lesson, the teacher displays an image of a spiral aloe plant on the board and asks students the following questions: 'What might this be?' 'How could it connect to maths?' 'Can you explain what you see using mathematical ideas?' The arrangement of the aloe's leaves demonstrates the Fibonacci sequence, making this a great starting point for engaging students and getting them to think laterally. It could be followed by further images showing the sequence in other settings.

Example 2: In a primary literacy lesson, the teacher displays an image of Goldilocks in the middle of a wanted poster. The poster bears (groan) the legend: 'Wanted for trespassing and stealing porridge.' Students are familiar with the Goldilocks story but have not thought about it in this way. The teacher poses a couple of questions for students to discuss: Has Goldilocks really committed a crime? How might the story be different if the bears were the main characters?

Counterintuitive Images

02 These images run against students' habits of thought. Their counterintuitive nature makes students look twice. Here is something which doesn't fit with expectations. Something unpredictable. And therefore something which needs to be thought about and engaged with.

Example 1: In an English lesson, the teacher displays three images on the board. These are up and ready so that students see them as soon as they enter the room. The first image is of Macbeth meeting the three wise men, the second is of Lady Macbeth advising the President of the United States and the third is of King Duncan wearing a dress. This is accompanied by the following question: To what extent is the play an expression of gender stereotypes?

Example 2: In a history lesson, the teacher displays a series of screen shots taken from the television version of 'The Man in the High Castle.' The screen shots are also placed on a handout and accompanied by a series of questions: Is counterfactual history worth thinking about? How might film and television influence the way in which we view the past? Is it the historian's job to think about what might have been, as well as what was? Why?

Images Which Need Unpicking

03 Unpicking an image means pulling it apart to reach a deeper meaning. Breaking it into pieces in an effort to understand what it shows and how it has been constructed. Images which need unpicking have something about them requiring further analysis. They might be complex, contrived, unusual or hard to fathom.

Example 1: In a primary numeracy lesson, the teacher starts the lesson by displaying an image of a fraction chart running from '1' to '1/12'. They ask students to look at the chart and to think about the following questions: How could we use the chart to help us? Can you break the chart down into separate sections? Who could use a chart like this in their job – and how would they use it?'

Example 2: In a geography lesson, the teacher displays a bird's eye image of London, overlaid with a grid dividing the image into six separate sections. The teacher assigns each section to a different group of students. They then ask the following questions: What does the image reveal about your section? How could you use your image to explain the benefits of bird's eye photography for geographers? What one thing from your section would you like to investigate in more detail, and why?

Unusual Sounds

04 A student walks into your classroom and hears an unusual sound. Something they weren't expecting and, maybe, have never heard before. Now you've got them. They're intrigued and want to know more.

Example 1: In a chemistry lesson, the teacher plays a looped recording of the noises made by fireworks exploding during a display. Students quickly realise what this is and the teacher reveals the lesson is about the chemistry involved in the manufacture of fireworks. Students are invited to listen to the sounds more closely and to think about the question: How might a chemist explain why different fireworks make different noises? In pairs, they make predictions and, through the course of the lesson, see whether or not these turn out to be correct.

Example 2: In a citizenship lesson, the teacher plays a recording of cars driving along a road. They pose the following question: What has this got to do with citizenship? Students discuss in pairs, their discussions underpinned by some uncertainty about what exactly is going on. The teacher asks a few students to share and then reveals the car noise was recorded directly outside the school...and that air pollution around schools is a pressing political issue in major cities throughout the country.

Musical Interlude

05 Music can conjure up a whole range of feelings and change the mood of a room. You can use this to start your lessons. Musical interludes set the tone from the moment students walk through the door.

Example 1: In a primary science lesson, the teacher is expecting students to come in with quite high energy levels, as this is directly after break. The lesson is going to involve extensive group work. Something the teacher knows works better if students are calmer. They think ahead and plan to have a Bach cello suite playing at the start of the lesson, knowing this calming influence will help bring order to proceedings, leading to better outcomes all round.

Example 2: In a classics lesson, the teacher starts things off by playing a selection of music from Ancient Rome. Students are invited to make comparisons between this and the music they listen to. The teacher encourages them to think about the role of music in their lives and to consider the role it might have played in Roman life. A collection of Roman instruments are displayed on the board, and students are invited to consider the relationship between technology and music – including how changes in the former might lead to changes in the latter.

Record Yourself

06 Because, hey, everybody's doing it, aren't they? Recording yourself means constructing an image of yourself via video. This has great potential for engaging students, challenging their preconceptions and changing the way your lessons normally start.

Example 1: In a PE lesson, the teacher takes an IPad onto the football field with them. They start the session by playing a video of themselves recorded the previous day. Students gather round and watch the teacher explaining how to use different parts of the foot when playing short and long passes. They then see the teacher deliberately getting things wrong as an exemplification of what not to do. The video finishes with the teacher telling students to get into pairs and to start practising.

Example 2: In an art lesson, the teacher plays a video of themselves demonstrating how to use watercolours to achieve a certain effect. They don't introduce the video or say anything about it. They just stand back and let students watch. When the video has finished playing, the teacher invites students to have a go themselves. Finally, the teacher leaves the video playing, looped and on mute, so students can refer to it while they are working.

Record Students

07 On the same theme, why not ask students to record themselves and then use this to start your lessons. There's lots of scope here for students working hard to outdo each other with exciting and unusual video intros to lessons. Creativity and a sense of agency are par for the course.

Example 1: In a primary history lesson, the teacher plays a video of a group of students re-enacting the Battle of Hastings. This was created in an earlier lesson, when the students worked with a teaching assistant outside the classroom. The teacher asks the class to identify key characters and events as they watch the video, and to be ready to discuss with a partner what they might have done differently if they had been making it.

Example 2: In a psychology lesson, the teacher kicks things off with a series of 60 second videos created by groups of students for their homework. Each video looks at the same topic from a different perspective, summarising the key points and ways of thinking connected to this. Students watch the videos in sequence and are then invited to discuss which approach they think is the best way of looking at this particular topic.

Record the Head

08 Taking the video idea down a different route altogether, try recording the head and using this video as the start of your lesson. There are some great opportunities for surprising students here – and for calling on the head's expertise, either as a subject specialist or as a go to person for behavioural issues.

Example 1: In a religious studies lesson, the teacher plays a video of the headteacher explaining about a trip they took to India, during the festival of Diwali. The headteacher is a religious studies specialist, and the video allows the teacher to tap into their experience while also bringing a different voice into the classroom through which to engage and interest their students.

Example 2: In a primary geography lesson, the teacher loads up a video of the headteacher sat in their office, looking sternly at the camera. They begin: 'Pupils of Class 4C, I have a mission I need you to complete. The government want me to deliver a report to them on volcanoes! They say I need to tell them everything there is to know about volcanoes, and that I have to do it by the end of the week. I need your help! Can you research volcanoes and tell me what I need to know by Friday?!'

YouTube

09 The world's stockpile of free-to-use video. There must be something on there you could use to start your lessons with a bang. Seriously. There's loads of great material. And you can use it in different ways as well. Perhaps to get students thinking in a certain direction, or maybe to challenge the thinking they did in the previous lesson.

Example 1: In a computing lesson, the teacher begins by playing a YouTube video showing cutting-edge technology produced by a team of MIT researchers (for example: https://www.youtube.com/watch?v=lvtfD_rJ2hE). They watch this with their students and then lead a discussion focussing on how the technology was created and the ways in which coding might have been used. This segues into the lesson proper, with students building on the discussion by writing their own code.

Example 2: In a biology lesson, the teacher begins by playing a YouTube video showing a widowbird jumping competition (https://www.youtube.com/watch?v=OPI-9oi19gQ). They watch this with their students and use it as a starting point for a discussion about natural selection and the role of sexual selection within the process of evolution. Students then go on to look at mating rituals in different species, comparing these to the jumping competition of the widowbirds.

Videos From Another World

10 Some videos take us to another world. One which is still on the Earth, but which is so different from our own lives that it draws us in like a light drawing the attention of a moth. These videos can create lesson starts that many students never forget.

Example 1: In a primary literacy lesson, the teacher plays a video of an Aboriginal dreamtime story. The teacher uses this as a way to start exploring Aboriginal storytelling. Students begin by watching the video and then through the discussion it provokes, before going on to look at different stories and some of the key tropes of this tradition. As part of this, the teacher leads students in making comparisons between Aboriginal storytelling and other forms with which they are familiar.

Example 2: In a music lesson, the teacher plays a clip from the film Baraka, in which we see Kecak, a form of Balinese dance and music drama (type 'Kecak into YouTube). The teacher makes no comment, simply letting students watch, listen and observe. When the performance is over, they prompt students to think about what they have seen. Then they show the video again. This time students are primed to analyse it – whereas on the first showing they were simply assimilating a completely new experience.

Social Media

11 For children today, social media is a ubiquitous presence. A permanent, if ever-changing, feature of their lives. Tap into this new reality by using social media as a vehicle through which to spark up engagement at the very start of your lessons.

Example 1: In a sociology lesson, the teacher asks students to take their phones out, go onto one or more of their social media accounts and think about the following questions: How are the norms and values different from real life? In what ways do people present themselves – and how is this different from real life? Where does status come from in the world of social media? Is this the same as the real world?

Example 2: In a physics lesson, the teacher sets up a Facebook group for their class and populates this with links to a range of videos, articles and experiments relevant to the current topic. The first ten minutes of the lesson sees students accessing the group on their mobile phones, and exploring the different links both individually and with peers. The teacher uses this as a way to get students thinking about the topic, before introducing it in a more formal manner.

Text/Tweet Me The Answer

12 Because most students will like being asked to get their smartphones out instead of being told to put them away! Plus, of course, this is an excellent way to quickly gain access to the thinking of most of the class. Though, of course, don't ask students to text your personal mobile number.

Example 1: In a design and technology lesson, the teacher pulls an empty box of cornflakes out of a bag, places it on the front desk and says: 'We need to redesign this packaging, and I want as many ideas as possible to get us started. Tweet your ideas to MrJones687 and use the hashtag #cerealdesign.' The teacher has set up the Twitter handle especially for the lesson. They log in and display on the whiteboard all the tweets coming in from students. This results in a whole-class brainstorm to get the lesson started.

Example 2: In a philosophy lesson, the teacher poses the question: 'Is it possible to say for certain that you know something to be true? Text me your answer.' They then display a mobile phone number on the board which refers to a cheap pay-as-you-go phone they bought for this purpose. When all the answers are in, they scroll through their phone, select one text at random, read it out and use this as the start of the discussion.

A Link, Just a Link

13 Displayed on the board. With nothing around it. And no explanation as to why it's there or what will happen when it's clicked. Then, you know, you just can't help wondering. What happens when we click the link? And there's only one way to satisfy such curiosity…

Example 1: In a primary numeracy lesson, the teacher displays a link on the board and then invites one student to come up to the front and click on it. When they do it reveals an online maths game in which the student has to correctly answer a series of sums in order to complete a level. The student who clicked the link gets to play while the rest of the class watch and shout out what they think are the right answers.

Example 2: In a government and politics lesson, the teacher displays three links on the board. These line up next to three differently coloured spots – one red, one blue and one green. The teacher asks the class to vote on which link they would like to click – red, blue or green. They conduct two different votes: first past the post and alternative votes. This has the benefit of exemplifying different voting systems at the same time as it engages students through the mystery of what lies behind the chosen link.

Google This!!

14 Students know how to use Google. They have their smartphones with them most of the time. So get them engaged and interacting right from the off by giving them something to Google. You can Google it yourself in advance to check what kind of information comes up.

Example 1: In a French lesson, the teacher displays a list of ten French words students are unlikely to have come across before. The first student to correctly translate all ten through Google is the winner. Alternatively, the teacher might display the names of three famous people from French history. Students have to Google these, choose the one they find most interesting, and then produce a short paragraph in French summarising why the person is famous.

Example 2: In a maths lesson, the teacher displays a famous equation on the board. Students have to Google this, find out what the equation is, how it is used and where it originally comes from. The teacher then presents students with a selection of real-world problems to which the equation is relevant and challenges them to find specific examples of each by searching through Google.

Snapshot

15 A picture is worth a thousand words. But what about a snapshot of a picture? Not the whole picture, just a little segment of it. With everything else blacked out. Leaving students to start wondering what, exactly, this snapshot is part of. What, exactly, is the bigger picture all about?

Example 1: In a primary art lesson, the teacher displays a snapshot of a pointillist picture. They ask pupils to look at this and to see if they can work out what is going on. Pupils are invited to come up to the board and to look more closely, to discuss with a partner and to think about what the bigger picture could be, as well as why it has been created using this technique. The teacher takes a number of answers – possibly using these to start a whole-class discussion – before revealing the full image.

Example 2: In an English lesson, the teacher displays a snapshot of a propaganda poster. Students can only see a small section of it – but one that includes a little portion of imagery, along with some text. The teacher invites the class to examine the snapshot and to see if they can work out what the full image is of. If students are finding this particularly difficult, the teacher can offer some prompts, hints or clues.

Stingray Questions

16 Like, what if World War Two had ended in 1940 with a unilateral ceasefire? Or, what if nuclear fusion could be effectively harnessed to meet domestic energy needs? Or, is a poem better, worse or the same if you don't know who the author is? Stingray questions pack a jolt, pushing students to think differently and more deeply.

Example 1: In a music lesson, the teacher plans a series of three stingray questions, each intended to challenge students to think more deeply about the topic: Is rhythm the same in different cultures? Do rhythms stop and start, or do we just stop playing them and start playing them? How could you use a series of rhythms to explain to me what rhythm is? These questions problematize students' conception of rhythm and act as an unusual way into the topic.

Example 2: In a primary science lesson, the teacher displays five stingray questions on the board, all connected to the topic. They invite pupils to look at these, discuss them with a partner and decide which they think is the most interesting. The class then votes on which question they would like to discuss. The teacher leads the discussion and, if there is time, helps pupils to explore the second most popular question as well.

Why X if Y?

17 As in: Why is seawater salty if freshwater isn't? Or: Why do Marxists want to overthrow capitalism if it has lifted so many people out of poverty? Or: Why do religious people pray if they don't necessarily expect to hear God talking back to them? Questions of this type bring together two premises and ask students to work out how they can be squared off with one another.

Example 1: In a history lesson, the teacher displays the following question on the board as students walk into the room: 'If many people knew the Treaty of Versailles could potentially cripple the German economy, then why did no one stop it from being signed?' Students are not yet familiar with the treaty, but the teacher wants them to know where the lesson, or unit, is going. They then display a second question: 'If the headteacher knew a punishment would have a bad effect on a student, why might she still go through with it anyway?'

Example 2: In a psychology lesson, the teacher displays three questions on the board: Why do some bystanders ignore people in need, even if they know it's the wrong thing to do? Why do many people cultivate a social media image even if they know it isn't the real them? Why do some people agree to things they know to be false when they find themselves in a large group? The teacher invites students to work in pairs, select one of the questions, discuss their thoughts, and plan an experiment they could use to find an answer.

Counterfactual Questions

18 Counterfactuals ask students to think about how the world might be different if certain facts were other than they are. This can knock students off their intellectual feet if pitched correctly at the beginning of a lesson… What if the Aztecs had invented seafaring and sailed to Europe fifty years before the Spanish set sail for South America?

Example 1: In a classics lesson, the teacher displays the following question on the board: 'What if the Roman Empire had survived beyond the 5th century and started to regain its previous power, wealth and scope?' This question becomes a lens through which to examine why the Empire did not survive, the influence it had on Europe despite its decline, and the way in which classics itself might be different if events had played out differently.

Example 2: In a physics lesson, the teacher displays the following three questions on the board: What if quantum physics had been discovered a hundred years earlier? What if our understanding of superconductivity was fifty years in advance of what it is? What if Newton had been born two centuries later? These questions give students the opportunity to think about the relationship between physics and the culture in which it is studied, practised and in which it develops. They do this by imagining a different culture, and maybe a different physics as a result.

BuzzFeed Lists

19 BuzzFeed is an internet news organisation that has a particular style. One with which many students will be familiar. And, even if they're not, aping this style can create some interesting, unusual and often funny starting points for your lessons.

Example 1: In a primary numeracy lesson, the teacher displays a slide containing the following text: 17 Things You Never Knew About Fractions. The lesson begins with the teacher revealing these 17 things, one-by-one. Each item on the list has its own slide, on which the text is written in a large, brightly-coloured font. Some slides have images complementing the text. The teacher increases engagement by delivering the facts in a TV-presenter style, using emphasis and dramatic pauses.

Example 2: In a government and politics lesson, the teacher displays a slide containing the following text: 13 Things That Only Happen in Liberal Democracies. They reveal the next slide…only, it's empty. Students are nonplussed. But then the teacher bounces the lesson onto them: 'OK, you have 5 minutes to create the list. Work with a partner. Time starts now!' When the time is up, the teacher selects a number of pairs to read out their lists. The class then vote on which one they think is best.

Hidden Questions

20 You must ask hundreds of questions every day. But, sometimes, don't you just wish there was another way? Well, there is. Hide a question – or a few questions – somewhere in your room. And then get students to find them at the start of the lesson!

Example 1: In a geography lesson, the teacher announces, right at the start, that five questions are hidden around the room. And that these questions need to be answered as part of the first activity. Students have 2 minutes to find the questions and bring them to the teacher. Chaos is likely to ensue! The teacher gives hints to help students find the questions and announces each time a question has been found and delivered to the front. Develop the activity by having a student on hand to type the questions up onto a PowerPoint slide as they are found.

Example 2: In a computing lesson, the teacher hands students a sheet containing three questions. Only, these questions are written in code. At the bottom of the sheet there is a key students can use to decode them. This is their first task. The second task is to answer the questions. And the third task is to write their own question, encode it, and then try it out on one of their peers.

Doorway Challenge

21 Here you are, walking down the corridor, same as ever. Coming into the classroom, as per usual. Except, this time, the teacher's standing there, handing out challenges to everyone. As soon as they walk through the door. This is a lesson that's a bit different. This is a lesson that stands out from the crowd!

Example 1: In a primary history lesson, the teacher hands pupils challenges as they enter the room. There are six challenges in all, meaning pupils can work independently or can find a partner or group to team up with. The teacher has two options here. They can write out a set of challenges, all of which are fairly similar in difficulty. Or, they can come up with a set of six challenges which get progressively more difficult. In the latter case, they can give certain challenges to certain students as a way of differentiating.

Example 2: In a citizenship lesson, students are handed a challenge as they walk through the door: 'You have five minutes to sketch out a campaign you could use to change how people think about fair trade. Work with a partner and imagine that money is no object.' Immediately, their energy is focussed and directed. Depending on how the activity plays out, the teacher might decide to let it run for longer than five minutes – but the initial time limit serves to sharpen minds.

Doorway Questions and Answers

22 Another way to get students up and running before they've even sat down is to hand out questions and answers. Only, some students get questions and some students get answers. They then have to begin the lesson by matching these up, and not stopping until the whole set of questions and answers have been matched up, checked and shown to you.

Example 1: In a chemistry lesson, the teacher has thirty students. They hand out fifteen questions and fifteen answers as students walk through the door. A slide is displayed on the board which reads: 'There is one right answer for every question. Your mission is to match up all the questions and answers. I want to see a line of matches around the edge of the classroom – then I will check to see if they are right!'

Example 2: In a religious studies lesson, the teacher has twenty students. They hand out ten questions and ten answers as students walk through the door. They explain that some questions have right answers and some don't! Students must work out which questions and answers match up, which answers are wrong, false or misleading, and, therefore, what the correct answers are to the remaining questions.

Doorway Mission

23 Our final doorway idea. Instead of challenges, questions or answers, why not missions? Your mission, if you choose to accept it, is to stand at your classroom door and hand students missions they have to complete at the beginning of your lesson. It's out of the ordinary and, for that very reason, is likely to drive engagement and get your lesson off to a great start.

Example 1: In a primary science lesson, the teacher hands students missions as they walk through the door. Every mission is the same. The slips of paper read: 'Your mission is to think of a way we can build the biggest bridge possible using only one newspaper, and nothing else! You can work on your own, with a partner or in a group. The newspapers are at the front of the room. Off you go!'

Example 2: In a sociology lesson, the teacher hands out a series of different missions as students walk through the door. These all relate to the main topic but involve students exploring it in different ways. The teacher indicates that students will need to share their findings once they have completed their missions so that everybody in the class has a chance to think about each different aspect of the topic.

Dress Up

24 Sherlock Holmes was one of my favourites. And when the students arrived they had to double take. Is this really happening? Is sir actually dressed up like Sherlock Holmes? Staying in character takes matters to another level. And students can't help but be engaged and excited by what's going on.

Example 1: In a philosophy lesson, the teacher dresses up as David Hume. They proceed to talk like David Hume and ask Hume-style questions to students. They interrogate students' responses in the manner of Hume and, if they feel they can pull it off, carry on playing Hume throughout the lesson. Much laughter is likely to ensue – as well as some raised eyebrows. But students will also be engaged from the off, unlikely to forget the lesson in a hurry and, of course, the role-play gives the teacher license to behave slightly differently from normal.

Example 2: In a biology lesson, the teacher dresses up as Charles Darwin. They explain who they are and invite students to ask them questions about their work on The Beagle, their theory of natural selection and their career more generally. This gives the teacher an opportunity to reveal their knowledge of Darwin's life and work, and help students to think about evolution in a different way.

Hand Out Props

25 As students enter the room, give some or all of them a prop. Don't tell them anything about this. Let them have a look at what you've provided. Let them play around with it and discuss it. Then, and only then, should you start to reveal what the prop is all about and what is coming next.

Example 1: In a primary literacy lesson, the teacher hands every pupils a sweet wrapper. Pupils are invited to explore these with a partner. To talk about them, to describe what the sweet once contained within tasted like, to imagine where they were made, where they were sold and where the sweets were eaten. They are then invited to start telling their own story of the sweet wrapper. This all forms the beginning of a creative writing activity over a sequence of lessons.

Example 2: In a German lesson, the teacher hands every fourth student an item they have brought home from their travels in Germany. Students are invited to explore the items in groups, to look at them, examine them and make some predictions about what they are for, how they are used and what they can tell us about Germany. The teacher uses this as a way to introduce a new topic as well as some key aspects of German culture.

Mystery Objects Await

26 Plant a mystery object on each desk in your classroom. Greet students at the door and tell them a mystery object awaits. Refuse all questions designed to find out what the object is. Give the mystery time to breathe. Watch how students respond. See what kind of engagement the mystery sows!

Example 1: In an art lesson, the teacher places ochre rocks on desks as the mystery objects. Students are invited to examine these, discuss them and consider what relevance they might have to the lesson. The teacher encourages students to share their rocks with each other so they might compare them and see whether all the mystery objects are similar, or whether they differ. After sufficient time has passed the teacher reveals that the rocks are used as the basis for pigments and paints in Aboriginal art. This lesson is the first in a unit looking at the topic.

Example 2: In a primary history lesson, the teacher places imitation World War Two ration books on desks and invites students to look at these. They display some supplementary questions on the board which students can use to structure their discussions. The teacher circulates through the room and offers hints, clues and prompts where appropriate. After sufficient time has passed they reveal where the ration books come from and how they were used, before introducing the topic of study as life at home during World War Two.

Crime Scene

27 Set up your classroom like a crime scene. Or, maybe, just rope off part of the room and call that the crime scene. After all, we all know what the usual response is when we see something like that. It's to take a look. Have a nosy. See what we can see. The crime scene draws us in...

Example 1: In an English lesson, the teacher ropes off a corner of the room. They place a series of suspicious items there, along with some handwritten notes. Some of these are clues – some are red herrings. Students find a piece of paper on their desks explaining that a crime has been committed (this connects to the text they are currently studying). Their mission is to work in teams of three. One person must go and examine the crime scene and report back to their group. The team should then try to work out what has happened, using their knowledge of the text to help them.

Example 2: In a history lesson, the teacher sets up a crime scene in the centre of the room. A series of forged documents are laid out on a table, alongside some quills and an ink well – the implication being that these were used to forge the documents. Students are invited to examine the crime scene. They are then given a copy of the forged documents (which relate to the topic of study) and asked to work with a partner to prove that these are false. They must call on their knowledge of the period to do so.

Mystery Lesson

28 As in, plan a lesson which doesn't fit with what you've been teaching. One which stands alone and has no apparent connection. And don't tell students about it. Just launch straight in. Let the mystery unfold in front of their eyes. And see how they react. Chances are they'll be engaged.

Example 1: In a PE lesson, the teacher brings out a sack of American footballs and proceeds to start teaching students how to throw like a quarterback. This has no relation to the ongoing scheme of work. The teacher doesn't explain why they are doing the lesson – they just get on and teach it. Students are surprised at first but are then drawn in by the novelty – and mystery – of doing something completely different.

Example 2: In a design and technology lesson, the teacher plans a lesson based on some of their work experience before they were a teacher. They happened to work as a costume designer in the theatre and so the lesson focuses on students designing and starting to make a costume for a production of their choice. Again, the novelty and mystery of the approach pulls students in, engaging them and leaving them wondering what is happening and why it is happening.

Secret Missions on Desks

29 So it seems like a normal lesson. But, wait. What's this in front of you? It's an envelope. With the words 'Secret Mission' written on the outside. You pick it up, turn it over and take out a slip of paper. As you start reading, your secret mission is revealed.

Example 1: In a primary numeracy lesson, students enter the room to find secret missions on their desks. The teacher has placed different missions on different desks in an effort to differentiate. They know from previous lessons that different students are at different stages with their ability to use fractions. All the secret missions relate to fractions, but the level of difficulty varies depending on which student the mission is for. The teacher circulates while students reveal their missions, ready to scaffold or model where necessary.

Example 2: In a music lesson, students enter the room and find secret missions on their desks – with these intended for groups of three or four students sat near each other. Three different secret missions are used. Each presents students with a task – they must work as a team to compose a piece of music which sits within a certain genre. A time limit is given, along with some supplementary instructions, guidance and possible starting points.

Sit on the Floor

30 At the front, at the back, or in the middle of the room. Sit on the floor and start the lesson. Don't mention what you're doing. Just do it. Start explaining what's going to happen and see how students react. The change in the routine will inevitably spark their thinking as they ask the question 'Why is Sir/Miss sitting on the floor?!'

Example 1: In a geography lesson, the teacher settles the class down and then sits on the floor at the back of the room. They start explaining that the lesson is about migration and that they are sat as a migrant might find themselves sat on a boat or in a lorry. By this point most of the class have turned round to look at the teacher. They then ask a student to play a video already cued up on the computer. This contains interviews with a range of refugees who have made perilous journeys to flee their countries of origin. All of this acts as a starting point for a discussion about migration and the human costs involved.

Example 2: In a primary religious studies lesson, the teacher sits down on the floor and invites the class to join them in a circle. Except, pupils must first work together to carefully clear the room of tables and chairs, so that there is enough space for everybody to sit. This acts as a starting point for a discussion about cooperation and working together. The teacher then leads the class in an exploration of how different religions value these ideas.

Remove the Chairs

31 Students enter the room and find there are no chairs. You can let them react or you can give instructions on what to do. Either way, the routine has been given a good shake and minds are sharpened, with attention focussed as a result.

Example 1: In a maths lesson, students enter the room and find there are no chairs. The teacher explains they've been stored next door. Students may go and get a chair if they can successfully solve a mathematical riddle which is displayed on the board. If students think they have solved the riddle they must attract the teacher's attention, tell them the solution (making sure no one else can hear) and wait to see if it is right or not. If it is, they can go and get a chair. If not, they must try again.

Example 2: In a psychology lesson, students enter the room and find there are no chairs. The teacher explains that the chairs are stored in an empty classroom next door. Students may go and get a chair if they can first devise a psychological experiment based on the premise that all the chairs have been removed from a room. The teacher suggests they might like to think about social influence and social psychology more generally – the area they are currently studying.

Remove the Tables

32 Even better than removing the chairs is removing the tables. Although it is harder to do. Again, students are faced with a dilemma as soon as the lesson begins: what is going on and how do I respond? They immediately have to start thinking.

Example 1: In a primary music lesson, all the tables have been stacked around the outside of the room. Pupils are given musical instruments with which to work and the teacher explains that the task is to come up with a piece of music associated with a certain feeling. No mention is made of the lack of tables, other than that pupils are not allowed to use them during their work. The effect is nothing more than creating a sense of novelty and difference to what students are usually used to.

Example 2: In a philosophy lesson, the teacher invites the class in. There is only one table, yet there are fourteen students. The teacher asks the class to devise the fairest way possible to decide who gets to sit at the table. A couple of caveats are thrown in: no more than four people are allowed to sit at the table; opting out is not an option – the table must have people sat at it. The exercise which follows acts as an experiential introduction to the analysis of fairness, justice and equality.

Three Envelopes on Each Desk

33 Instead of leaving a single envelope on students' desks. Containing, for example, a secret mission. Leave three envelopes. Each with a different mission inside. Label the envelopes A, B and C. Then invite students to choose one – and only one – to form the basis of their efforts over the next 5-10 minutes.

Example 1: In a physics lesson, the teacher places three envelopes on each desk. Envelope A contains an experimental task, Envelope B asks students to create a thinking map for the topic, and Envelope C has a selection of exam questions to which students must produce model answers. The teacher asks all students to make their selections at the same time. This avoids the situation arising where some students wait to see what the envelopes contain by observing their peers.

Example 2: In a computing lesson, the teacher follows a similar approach, except the envelopes are replaced by three Word documents stored on the school's shared area and labelled 'A', 'B' and 'C'. Each one contains a different task for students to complete. The teacher tells students where the documents are stored and then invites them to select one at random to form the basis of the work they do during the start of the lesson. The teacher circulates while this is happening to offer support – and to make sure students don't wait to see what is behind each letter before making their choice.

Lucky Dip

34 It's a bit like tombola at the fair. Create a lucky dip from which students have to select something at random. This could be one student selecting on behalf of the whole class, or it could be every student selecting their own lucky dip. The uncertainty – and the potential – make this engaging.

Example 1: In a biology lesson, the teacher brings out a box covered in shiny wrapping paper. In this box are a series of different pieces of paper, folded over and with a different task written on each. The teacher invites one student to come to the front of the room and to select a piece of paper at random from the box. They read out the task which is written on this and it forms the basis of the starter activity for the whole class.

Example 2: In a citizenship lesson, the teacher stands at the door, holding a bag containing thirty pieces of paper, each folded over and with a task or question connected to the topic written on them. As students enter the room they reach inside the bag and pick out a piece of paper at random. The task or question written on their piece of paper forms the basis of their starter activity.

Fortune Cookies

35 There are online companies who will make fortune cookies for you. With your own messages printed up to go inside. Ah! The possibilities are endless. Though do check for any food intolerances. In fact, you might decide that students should only break open the fortune cookies to find out what's inside, and not actually eat them as well.

Example 1: In a Spanish lesson, the teacher hands out a set of fortune cookies. Inside each is a piece of paper with a question written in Spanish. Students must break open their fortune cookies, read the question, translate it, and then work out how they could answer it. When they've done this, they should pose the question to two or three of their peers. This sees the activity developing into a full-scale speaking and listening exercise.

Example 2: In an art lesson, the teacher hands out a set of fortune cookies. Inside each is a piece of paper with a different theme written on it. Students must break open their fortune cookies to reveal what theme they need to pursue in their painting during the course of the lesson. The teacher invites students to discuss their themes with a partner and, as part of this discussion, to think about ways they might render them in paint.

Real-World Problems

36 Take a look at the newspaper. What real-world problems are people grappling with? Use one or more of these as a way to start your lesson. It's about bringing the outside world into the classroom. And engaging students in the process.

Example 1: In a design and technology lesson, the teacher shares a story about a hydroelectric dam being built in Scotland. They explain the basic design of the dam and the way in which it will be used to generate electricity, before going on to outline some of the potential problems and difficulties caused by its design and construction. Students are invited to discuss different ways in which these could be overcome – and to think about how design can be used to create more effective technology in general.

Example 2: In a primary literacy lesson, the teacher starts by sharing a news story about a litter problem in the local area. They talk to pupils about the story and ask them what they think about it. Pupils look at pictures of the affected area and discuss what they think should be done. The teacher then explains that persuasive writing and speaking are important ways to change people's minds about a problem. The lesson focuses on using these to influence local opinion.

Compelling Stories

37 Stories draw us in. Compelling stories capture our attention. We want to know what happens next. We have to know what happens next. So we listen, or read, with the express intention of finding out. And what better way could there be to engage students at the very start of a lesson?

Example 1: In a PE lesson, the teacher begins by telling students the story of Jesse Owens, the African-American athlete who won four gold medals at the 1936 Olympics – the so-called Nazi games. The teacher uses the story to show how sport can transcend itself and have a political impact. They also use it to explain how Owens trained, and why he was so successful. This engages students and inspires them to put maximum effort into the lesson.

Example 2: A classics teacher uses Greek myths as starting points for a number of lessons. The stories possess compelling narratives which draw students in, engaging them as soon as the lessons begin. By using a series of myths over a number of lessons, the teacher habituates students into expecting this kind of lesson start. They thus arrive at the classroom anticipating that they will hear a story – meaning they are primed for engagement from the moment they walk through the door.

Last Night's News

38 Because it happened last night, and now we're in the lesson the next day and we're suddenly being asked to discuss it. So, like, that's really topical, isn't it? And relevant. And interesting.

Example 1: In a primary citizenship lesson, the teacher begins by sharing a story about the NHS. They scaffold this with questions helping pupils to talk first about their own experiences of the health service, and then about their ideas of fairness. The discussion develops into an examination of what makes something fair. This is then used to examine how the government makes public spending decisions. For example, whether money should go on schools, hospitals or something else.

Example 2: In a government and politics lesson, the teacher begins by sharing a news story from the previous night about the latest machinations in parliament. The class is divided in half. One half must come up with arguments which support the government's view on the story while the other half must come up with arguments which support the opposition's view. To make this harder, the teacher first asks students to say who they agree with. Students are then asked to defend the side with which they disagree.

Read Aloud

39 There's just something about hearing someone read aloud – especially when it's done well, with emphasis, clarity and feeling. We have to listen. Like with any story, we want to know what happens next. So we keep listening. And before we know it, the lesson is in full swing and we're rapt.

Example 1: In a sociology lesson, the teacher begins by reading an extract from a criminal's autobiography. They choose a compelling section and start reading it without giving students any warning of what is happening or why. Students are gripped by the narrative and want to know what happens next. When the teacher finishes, they give out copies of the extract and use these as stimulus for a discussion about the causes of crime.

Example 2: In a primary geography lesson, the teacher begins by reading aloud an extract from a book about what it is like to live next to the Amazon River. Students are immediately engaged and want to know more. The teacher continues for as long as feels right – they have to take a reading of the room to ascertain when they have gone on for long enough. The lesson then focuses on the river more generally, with students exploring the topic from various different perspectives.

Podcast

40 Creating a podcast is easy. You just need to record your own voice, upload this and share it with students. You can move things on by interviewing people as part of your podcast. Or, you could just select a segment of an existing podcast to start with.

Example 1: In a chemistry lesson, the teacher books a computer room and shares with students a podcast they have made. The podcast talks students through the topic of genetic variation. As part of this, it guides them to a number of relevant websites, telling them where to find specific resources and further explanations. The podcast lasts around fifteen minutes. Students listen to it for the first fifteen minutes of the lesson; then the teacher takes over and the lesson moves forwards.

Example 2: In a history lesson, the teacher plays a selection from an existing podcast in which an interviewer discusses Henry VIII with a well-known historian of the Tudor period. The teacher supplements this with a series of questions students can use to think about and critique what they are hearing. When the selection has finished playing, the teacher invites students to discuss their answers to these questions with a partner before leading a whole-class discussion on the topic.

Arrange to Receive a Call

41 Two minutes into the lesson and your phone (which you've turned up to full volume) starts blaring out. You've arranged to receive a call – but the students don't know that. So you take the call and make it look like it changes the course of the entire lesson. Great interest abounds as a result.

Example 1: In a maths lesson, the teacher receives a call after two minutes. They answer their phone, listen for a moment, give their assent and then end the call. They turn to the class and announce that the lesson has to be changed. Instead of looking at trigonometry and the construction of triangles, it is imperative they study probability instead. Of course, the teacher always intended this – but the students don't know that and so the sudden change of tack feels surprising and engaging.

Example 2: In an English lesson, the teacher receives a call two minutes in. They have a conversation with the person on the other end of the line before abruptly ending the call. They turn to the class and explain that instead of reading the next chapter in their class book, they have been asked to write a new chapter themselves. A chapter which they must then compare against the original, to see how similar or different their ideas are.

Arrange to Receive a Visit

42 Instead of a call, why not a visit? Arrange for a helpful colleague to interrupt your lesson just as you're getting started. They should deliver news which (so it appears) fundamentally alters what you have planned. Students think they're in on the game but, in reality, you've contrived things to make life a little more interesting for them.

Example 1: In a primary literacy lesson, a colleague enters the room a few minutes after the start. They say they are bringing urgent news. The head teacher needs a story they can use that afternoon when they cover one of the reception classes. It must be about a magic box and it should have a happy ending. The class need to get started on it straightaway! The colleague leaves and the teacher takes over.

Example 2: In a religious studies lesson, a colleague enters the room near the start of the lesson and engages in what appears to be a whispered conversation with the class teacher. The conversation ends and the colleague leaves the room. The class teacher then announces that the lesson has to be changed. They give no reason for this but intimate that it is vitally important. PowerPoint slides are swapped over and the real lesson is revealed.

Time Limit

43 Thirty seconds to answer the question. 42 seconds to attempt the problem. One minute and nine seconds to find out what three people in the room think. Time limits up the pace and drive student decision-making. This can be a great way to get energy levels up at the beginning of a lesson.

Example 1: In a psychology lesson, the teacher displays three questions on the board and explains that discussion of these will form the start of the lesson. They then announce a time limit: sixty seconds per question. A countdown timer is displayed and the teacher hurries students along. At the end of the three minutes, the teacher leads a whole-class discussion in which various students share their thoughts.

Example 2: In a biology lesson, the teacher gives students a task to complete in the first seven minutes. The task is broken down into three separate sections. The teacher indicates that these should take two minutes, three minutes and two minutes to complete. A countdown timer is displayed and the teacher circulates through the room, chivvying students along and reminding them of how much time is left. When the time is up, students share their work with one another.

Multiple Time Limits

44 And why not use a series of time limits, one after the other. This way, you can wind up the pace, getting students to act and think more and more quickly. Used carefully, this can take the pace to a frenetic level, meaning your lesson really starts with a bang!

Example 1: In a primary numeracy lesson, the teacher displays a set of five sums on the board. Pupils have two minutes to work through these with a partner. When the time is up, the answers are revealed and pupils mark their own work. Then, the teacher displays another set of five sums. This time, however, pupils only have ninety seconds to complete them. The exercise is repeated twice more, culminating in a thirty second race against the clock.

Example 2: In a citizenship lesson, the teacher displays an exam question on the board as a starter activity. They announce that students have two minutes to answer it, start the countdown timer and tell students to begin. When the time is up, they reveal a second question – of the same type but with different content. For this, students have only ninety seconds. Finally, a third question is revealed, and students must try to answer it in sixty seconds.

Procedural Challenges

45 This is where we challenge students to complete procedural tasks with ever-increasing levels of efficiency. The idea is to get students working together at the start of the lesson, having some fun and experiencing success in a low-stakes setting. This creates a positive atmosphere from which to work.

Example 1: In a primary design and technology lesson, the teacher sets pupils the procedural challenge of setting up the working area, ready for the lesson. A series of sub-tasks are displayed on the board: (i) Everybody must be wearing an apron. (ii) All tables must be covered with newspaper. (iii) All materials should be shared equally between the class. The challenge is to do all of this as quickly, quietly and efficiently as possible. The teacher records how long it takes so pupils can try and beat their time on the next occasion.

Example 2: In a PE lesson, the teacher sets students the procedural challenge of setting up a series of five-a-side football pitches using cones and movable goals. They divide the class into three teams, turning the challenge into a competition. The team who correctly set up their pitch first are the winners.

Lesson Start Race

46 Why not turn the start of your lesson into a race? Set students off on a series of tasks they need to complete to start the lesson. But emphasise that this is a race – and the winner will be the person who completes the tasks quickest...but also to a requisite standard.

Example 1: In a primary history lesson, the teacher displays three tasks on the board. They explain that pupils' have to complete these as quickly as possible, but that they must complete them to a high standard. To ensure this happens, the teacher also displays three lots of success criteria – one lot per task. Pupils must meet these for their attempts to be deemed successful. The first pupil to claim they have finished all three tasks must have their work checked by the teacher, who is the final arbiter.

Example 2: In a chemistry lesson, the teacher displays a set of seven equations which need balancing. They announce that this is a race to start the lesson. The first student to complete the equations will be the winner. However, the teacher stresses, the equations must be completed correctly. Anyone who finishes but has got some of their equations wrong will automatically be ruled out of winning!

Human Jigsaw

47 Give every student in your class a piece of the puzzle, and then ask the class to put those pieces together. This creates a human jigsaw. Meaning all students are engaged from the off. They have to think, interact, communicate and work as a team as soon as you tell them to begin.

Example 1: In a German lesson, the teacher gives every student a slip of paper as they enter the room. Half the class receive pieces of paper with German words written on them. The rest of the class receive pieces of paper containing the English equivalents of the German words. The teacher explains the situation and then invites students to match up the German and English words. When the whole class believes they have successfully matched all the words, the teacher works through each pairing to see whether they are right or not.

Example 2: In a computing lesson, the teacher gives every student a slip of paper as they enter the room. Each piece of paper contains a section of code. Students are challenged to reassemble the code in full, using every piece of paper. The teacher observes as students try to complete the task. When they believe they are done the teacher is called over to check whether they have been successful or not.

Team Challenge

48 Divide the class into teams as they come into the room. Then quickly reveal a team challenge. Something every team has to do – and for which there can only be one winner: the team who finishes fastest.

Example 1: In a primary science lesson, the teacher divides the class into eight teams. They display the following challenge on the board: Your mission is to create a poster explaining how people can have a positive effect on the environment. You have ten minutes. Your poster must include at least three positive effects, it must have pictures as well as words, and it should include examples from our local area. The team who finishes first, who meet the success criteria, and who make the best job possible, will be the winners!

Example 2: In a government and politics lesson, the teacher divides the class into five teams. They display a statement on the board: 'Liberty is best protected by a strong state.' The teacher announces that the challenge is to identify how five different theories might respond to this statement: liberalism, feminism, anarchism, conservatism, and socialism. The first team to correctly identify five different responses are the winners.

Sound the Alarm

49 Get an alarm noise from the internet (or bring in a real alarm) and sound it to signal a sudden change in the start of the lesson. You can even signal the alarm on multiple occasions in order to change students' focus 2, 3 or even 4 times.

Example 1: In a physics lesson, the teacher sets students off on a standard starter activity. After a couple of minutes they sound the alarm and announce that the topic of the lesson has changed. A second starter activity is introduced. The teacher repeats the process on a further two occasions. Then, after students have completed the fourth starter activity, the teacher reveals a slide showing how all the activities actually link together and that, far from these being four separate topics, they are in fact four aspects of the same topic – on which the lesson as a whole will focus.

Example 2: In a geography lesson, the teacher asks students to create a model exam answer as a starter activity. Half-way through this, they sound the alarm and announce that the task has changed. Students must now answer a similar exam question in timed conditions. After they have done this, the alarm sounds a third time. Now, students must annotate their answers with the thinking which underpinned them. The alarm then sounds for a fourth and final time. Students must now compare their annotated answers with the model answers they first produced – and with the work of a partner.

Take it Outside

50 Because everybody loves leaving the classroom and having a lesson outside. Unless the weather is really, really bad. Then it might be better to stay inside. But you could still go outside the classroom. To the hall, for example, or the corridor. Or even the canteen. Where you could make a bad joke about being hungry for knowledge.

Example 1: In a philosophy lesson, the teacher gives students a handout containing a table. Column one lists a series of school locations: the vending machine, the tennis courts, reception, the library and so on. The following question heads column two: How might Marxists interpret this? The teacher takes the class on a tour of the school, visiting each location in turn. At each point, the teacher outlines how Marxist doctrine might be applied to the location in question. Students capture the information on their sheets as they go.

Example 2: In a primary art and design lesson, the teacher tells pupils that instead of drawing from memory, they are going to go out into the school grounds and draw from real life. The teacher gives pupils a set of areas they can choose from: the playground, the football pitch, the allotment, the herb garden and the steps. They are allowed to visit each area when the class is outside before deciding which one they will use as the basis of their drawing.

And with that, we draw our journey to a close. I hope you've found the ideas in the book interesting – and that you can see ways in which to adapt them for your learners and the subject or age group you teach. Some of the best lessons I've ever taught started with strategies included in this book – and some of the most fun as well. So let me finally conclude by saying I hope you enjoy implementing some of the ideas – and that you and your students have a lot of fun along the way.

A Brief Request

If you have found this book useful I would be delighted if you could leave a review on Amazon to let others know.

If you have any thoughts or comments, or if you have an idea for a new book in the series you would like me to write, please don't hesitate to get in touch at mike@mikegershon.com.

Finally, don't forget that you can download all my teaching and learning resources for **FREE** at www.mikegershon.com and www.gershongrowthmindsets.com

Printed in Great Britain
by Amazon